30
Days of
Learning
Islamic
Expressions

Copyright © 2022 Goodhearted Books Inc.
info@goodheartedbooks.com

ISBN: 978-1-988779-58-4

Dépôt légal : bibliothèque et archives nationales du Québec, 2022.
Dépôt légal : bibliothèque et archives Canada, 2022.

Created by   : Bachar Karroum
Graphic Designer   : Samuel Gabriel
Cover Designer   : Creative Hands
Content revision   : Mohammed Achkanou, Safa Said, Mohamed Ali
Proofreader   : Christine Campbell

IN THE NAME OF ALLAH

Bringing this practical book to life for you and your little ones has been an inspiring journey. We are grateful to be able to build on our series of books, to share the essence of Islam with our kids. This creation has been specially crafted to shine a light on the amazing Islamic expressions.

We hope that you and your family members will enjoy this learning experience and that it will help your children become the best versions of themselves while spreading the beautiful values of our beloved religion.

TO KNOW BEFORE YOU START

To improve the pronunciation of some expressions, we use the following symbols:

♡ ā: to extend the pronunciation of the letter "a". Ex: Bismillāh

♡ ʿa: to replace the Arabic letter "ع". Ex: Assalāmu ʿalaykum

♡ ū: to extend the pronunciation of the letter "u". Ex: Aʿūdhu billāh

GLOSSARY

♡ PBUH : Peace be upon him

IN THE NAME OF ALLAH

بسم الله

Bismillāh

MEANING OF THIS EXPRESSION

It means "In the name of God". Muslims commonly use this expression before starting any activity or good action.

HOW CAN I USE IT?

Start everything with "Bismillāh," like before eating or doing your homework. It'll give you the blessing of Allah in your day.

DAY 1

PRAISE BE
TO ALLAH

الحمد لله

Alhamdulillāh

MEANING OF THIS EXPRESSION

It means "Thank God." Muslims commonly use this expression to express gratitude and appreciation toward Allah for whatever happens in their lives.

HOW CAN I USE IT?

You can say "Alhamdulillāh" on every occasion, like when you finish eating, sneezing, or waking up. Always remember to say it, as it's the best way to thank Allah.

DAY 2

IF ALLAH
WILLS

إنشاء الله

Inshā Allāh

MEANING OF THIS EXPRESSION

It means we accept that nothing can happen without Allah's will. Muslims commonly use this expression after a promise, intention, or to add Allah's blessing to their plans.

HOW CAN I USE IT?

Make a habit of saying "Inshā Allāh" each time you tell your friends or parents about something you intend to do. It'll bless your action and make things easier with Allah's help.

DAY 3

GLORY BE
TO ALLAH

سبحان الله

Subhānallāh

MEANING OF THIS EXPRESSION

It means "Allah is Perfect." Muslims commonly use this expression to express the feeling of amazement by Allah's creations.

HOW CAN I USE IT?

You can say "Subhānallāh" when you see any of Allah's wonderful creations, like a lovely view, a cute baby, a beautiful animal, or a tiny insect.

DAY 4

WHAT ALLAH HAS WILLED

ما شاء الله

Mā shā Allāh

MEANING OF THIS EXPRESSION

It means "We surrender to Allah's will." Muslims commonly use it to express a feeling of awe after seeing fabulous things. Some Muslims say it to protect themselves from jealousy or evil eyes when something good happens.

HOW CAN I USE IT?

You can use this expression whenever you see a skill, a force, or a beautiful quality in a friend. For example: "Mā shā Allāh, you have an amazing talent in sport, Fatima."

DAY 5

ALLAH IS THE GREATEST

الله أكبر

Allāhu akbar

It means God is the supreme authority. Muslims commonly use it to express the greatness of Allah over everything. It's also used to express happiness, for something great has just happened.

HOW CAN I USE IT?

You can say "Allāhu akbar" during your daily prayers; whenever you feel happy about having good news; or when seeing something unique or powerful.

DAY 6

PEACE BE UPON YOU

السلام عليكم

Assalāmu ʿalaykum

MEANING OF THIS EXPRESSION

It's a traditional greeting among Muslims. They pronounce it when arriving or leaving a gathering, just as we say hi and goodbye in English.

HOW CAN I USE IT?

You can say "Assalāmu 'alaykum" when you leave your house in the morning or meet your friends at school. Make sure your friends understand Arabic.

DAY 7

I SEEK THE FORGIVENESS OF ALLAH

استغفر الله

Astaghfirullāh

MEANING OF THIS EXPRESSION

It's a short Dua that Muslims commonly use to ask forgiveness from Allah for their sins or mistakes.

HOW CAN I USE IT?

Allah likes those who ask for forgiveness. Every time you think you acted wrongly, say "Astaghfirullāh." Allah is the best forgiver.

MAY ALLAH BLESS YOU

بارك الله فيك

Bārakallāhu fik

MEANING OF THIS EXPRESSION

It means "God bless you." Muslims commonly use this expression to express gratitude and appreciation to someone they are talking with.

HOW CAN I USE IT?

When thanking a friend who helped you or gave you a hand, you can say, "Bārakallāhu fik." Make sure your friend understands Arabic.

(BE) WITH THE
SAFETY OF ALLAH

في أماني الله

Fi amanillāh

MEANING OF THIS EXPRESSION

It means to be in the protection of Allah. Muslims commonly use this expression to say goodbye to someone.

HOW CAN I USE IT?

You can say this expression to someone who is leaving. For example: "Fi amanillāh. Have a safe flight, dad!" or "Fi amanillāh. Have a great day at work, mom!"

DAY 10

IN THE CAUSE
OF ALLAH

في سبيل الله

Fi sabilillāh

MEANING OF THIS EXPRESSION

It means the good deeds we're doing are for the sake of Allah. Muslims commonly use this expression when giving charity or helping others.

HOW CAN I USE IT?

You can say "Fi sabilillāh" to encourage your friends to do good deeds. For example, you can say: "Let's gather some clothes we don't use and give them, Fi sabilillāh, to the needy."

DAY 11

ALLAH IS SUFFICIENT FOR US AND THE BEST OF THOSE ON WHOM TO DEPEND

حسبنا الله
و نعم الوكيل

Hasbunallāhu wa
ni'mal-wakil

MEANING OF THIS EXPRESSION

It means Allah is enough for us when we have a problem. He is our best protector. Muslims commonly use this expression when facing a difficult situation and are seeking Allah's help.

HOW CAN I USE IT?

You can say it whenever you feel worried about a situation you can't control. For example, "Mom told me if the new virus persists, many people will suffer." You can reply with: "Hasbunallāhu wa ni'mal-wakil."

WE BELONG TO ALLAH, AND TO HIM, WE SHALL RETURN

إنا لله وإنا
إليه راجعْون

Inna lillāhi wa
innā ilayhi raji'un

MEANING OF THIS EXPRESSION

It means we belong to Allah, and we will return to Him. Muslims commonly use this expression when they learn about someone who just passed away.

HOW CAN I USE IT?

You can say "Inna lillāhi wa innā ilayhi raji'un" whenever you hear about someone passing away. It'll bring you patience and help you cope with the situation.

DAY 13

MAY ALLAH REWARD YOU WITH GOODNESS

جزاك الله خيراً

Jazāk Allāhu
khayran

MEANING OF THIS EXPRESSION

It means "May Allah give you good things in life." Muslims commonly use this expression in conversation to express thankfulness or gratitude to the person with whom they are talking.

HOW CAN I USE IT?

You can say "Jazāk Allāhu khayran" to thank a friend for something good he has done for you. Make sure your friend understands Arabic.

DAY 14

THERE IS NO POWER, NO STRENGTH, EXCEPT WITH ALLAH

لا حول ولا
قوة إلا بالله

Lā hawla wala
quwwata illā billāh

MEANING OF THIS EXPRESSION

It means that only through Allah can we have strength and power. Muslims commonly use this expression when they feel weak about a situation and seek strength and power through Allah's help.

HOW CAN I USE IT?

You can say "Lā hawla wala quwwata illā billāh" whenever you're scared. It will give you courage and make your heart remember that Allah is the most powerful.

THERE IS NO GOD BUT ALLAH; MOHAMMAD IS THE MESSENGER OF ALLAH

لا إله إلا الله
محمد رسول الله

Lā ilāha illā Allāh
Mohammad rasoolullāh

MEANING OF THIS EXPRESSION

It means Allah is the only God, and the Prophet Mohammad (PBUH) is His last messenger. It's one of the five pillars of Islam. Muslims use it to confirm their faith in Islam.

HOW CAN I USE IT?

You can say "Lā ilāha illā Allāh Mohammad rasoolullāh" whenever you want. It'll increase your love for Allah and His Prophet (PBUH), reinforce your faith, and reduce your daily worries.

DAY 16

ALLAH FORBID

لا سمح الله

Lā samahallāh

MEANING OF THIS EXPRESSION

It means "May Allah not let a negative situation occur." Muslims commonly use this expression during a conversation, hoping to avoid something negative from happening.

HOW CAN I USE IT?

When you are describing a potentially negative situation, you would say this expression in the hope of avoiding this event from occurring. For example: "If dad loses his job, Lā samahallāh, it'll be hard for the whole family."

DAY 17

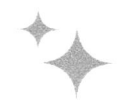

I SEEK REFUGE
IN ALLAH

أعوذ بالله

A`ūdhu billāh

MEANING OF THIS EXPRESSION

It means to seek protection from Allah. Muslims commonly use this expression to seek refuge in Allah against evil.

HOW CAN I USE IT?

You can say "A`ūdhu billāh" in the context of seeking Allah's protection from a false accusation. For example, if someone accuses you of lying to your parents, you can reply with: "A`ūdhu billāh. I would never lie to my parents."

DAY 18

MAY ALLAH BE PLEASED WITH HIM

رضي الله عنه

Radiyallāhu ʿanh

MEANING OF THIS EXPRESSION

It means "May Allah be pleased with him."
Muslims commonly use this expression when pronouncing or hearing the name of one of the companions of Prophet Mohammad (PBUH).

HOW CAN I USE IT?

You can say "Radiyallāhu 'anh" whenever you hear the name of Prophet Mohammad's (PBUH) companion. It's a great way to show them respect.
For example: "Abu Bakr Radiyallāhu 'anh."

DAY 19

PEACE BE UPON HIM

صلى الله عليه وسلم

Sallallāhu 'alayhi
wa sallam

MEANING OF THIS EXPRESSION

It means "May Allah honor the Prophet Mohammad and grant him peace." Muslims commonly use this expression whenever they mention or hear the name of the Prophet Mohammad (PBUH).

HOW CAN I USE IT?

Make a habit of saying "Sallallāhu 'alayhi wa sallam" whenever you mention or hear someone mention the name of Prophet Mohammad (PBUH). It's a great habit to show him love and respect.

DAY 20

THE MOST GLORIFIED, THE MOST HIGH

سبحانه وتعالى

Subhanahu wa ta'ālā

MEANING OF THIS EXPRESSION

It means "All glory belongs to Allah. He is the highest, the most exalted, the absolute, and perfect." Muslims often use this expression when they mention Allah to glorify His name.

HOW CAN I USE IT?

Make a habit of saying "Subhanahu wa ta'ālā" whenever you pronounce or hear someone mention Allah Almighty. It's a noble habit to show Him love and respect.

DAY 21

I PUT MY FAITH IN THE HANDS OF ALLAH

توكلت على الله

Tawakkaltu 'alallāh

MEANING OF THIS EXPRESSION

It means trusting in Allah's plan.

Muslims commonly use this expression to bring positivity to their lives or to calm themselves in stressful situations.

HOW CAN I USE IT?

Make a habit of saying "Tawakkaltu 'alallāh" every morning and every night before sleeping. Asking for Allah's support is the best way to have a positive life.

DAY 22

OH ALLAH!

يا الله

Yā Allāh

MEANING OF THIS EXPRESSION

It means we believe in Allah's presence. Muslims commonly use it when they're amazed by something, when they're calling for Allah's help, when they're hurting, or when they are worried about something.

HOW CAN I USE IT?

You can say "Yā Allāh" whenever you need to feel Allah's presence. It can be when you're worried or sad. For example: "Yā Allāh, please help me through this challenging period."

MAY ALLAH HAVE MERCY ON YOU

يرحمك الله

Yarhamukallāh

MEANING OF THIS EXPRESSION

It means "May Allah bless you and have compassion on you." Muslims commonly use this expression when hearing someone sneeze. It's like saying "God bless you" in English.

HOW CAN I USE IT?

You can say "Yarhamukallāh" whenever a friend or family member sneezes.

DAY 24

MAY ALLAH GUIDE YOU

يهديكم الله

Yahdikumullāh

MEANING OF THIS EXPRESSION

It means "may Allah show you the right path." Muslims commonly use this expression when someone tells them "Yarhamukallāh" after sneezing. It's like saying "thank you" when someone tells you "bless you."

HOW CAN I USE IT?

You can reply by "Yahdikumullāh" when someone tells you "Yarhamukallāh" after sneezing.

DAY 25

MAY ALLAH ENNOBLE HIS FACE

كرم الله وجهه

Karramallāhu wajhah

MEANING OF THIS EXPRESSION

It means "May Allah honor him." Muslims commonly use this expression when pronouncing or hearing Imam Ali's name.

HOW CAN I USE IT?

Make a habit of saying this expression whenever you pronounce or hear someone mention Imam Ali's name (Imam Ali "Karramallāhu wajhah"). It's a great habit to show him respect.

MAY THE MERCY OF ALLAH BE UPON HIM

رحمة الله عليه

Rahmatullāhi ʿalayh

MEANING OF THIS EXPRESSION

It means "May Allah show him grace." Muslims commonly use this expression whenever they talk about or remember a loved one who passed away. It's like the English term "May he rest in peace."

HOW CAN I USE IT?

You can say "Rahmatullāhi 'alayh" whenever you talk about or remember a loved one who has passed away.

DAY 27

MAY ALLAH ACCEPTS

تقبل الله

Taqabbala Allāh

MEANING OF THIS EXPRESSION

It means "May Allah receive your prayers." Muslims commonly use this expression when they see someone who has just finished their prayers.

HOW CAN I USE IT?

Make a habit of saying "Taqabbala Allāh" whenever you see one of your family members finish their prayers.

DAY 28

IT IS THE DECREE OF ALLAH, AND HE DOES WHATEVER HE WILLS

قدر الله و ما شاء فعل

Qaddarallāhu wa
mā shāa fa`al

MEANING OF THIS EXPRESSION

It means we accept what Allah has decided of a situation for us. Muslims commonly use this expression to reinforce their patience during challenging circumstances.

HOW CAN I USE IT?

You can say this when you feel sad about a situation you didn't want to happen. For example, when you hear the news about an earthquake in your country, you can say: "Qaddarallāhu wa mā shāa fa`al."

DAY 29

ALLAH GIVES TIME BUT NEVER NEGLECTS

يمهل ولا يهمل

Yumhilu wa lā yuhmil

MEANING OF THIS EXPRESSION

It means that Allah has time for your prayers and never abandons them. Muslims commonly use this expression when impatiently waiting for an answer to their prayers.

HOW CAN I USE IT?

You can say "Yumhilu wa lā yuhmil" to someone who feels their prayers have not yet been answered. It'll make them remember that Allah is not neglecting them. He wants us to be patient.

PRAY UPON THE PROPHET MOHAMMAD

صلِّ على النبي

Salli 'ala nabi

MEANING OF THIS EXPRESSION

It means to pray for blessings on the Prophet Mohammad (PBUH). Muslims commonly use this expression to calm down a situation or send positive vibes during a conversation.

HOW CAN I USE IT?

Make a habit of saying "Salli 'ala nabi" whenever you see your dad or mom angry or in a bad mood. This will comfort them and make them relax.

DAY 31

We sincerely hope that you enjoyed this book.
We worked diligently to bring to light the essential values of Islam to help
our children fulfill their highest potential.

If you believe we can further enhance our content, please
don't hesitate to contact us at :

info@goodheartedbooks.com

Otherwise, feel free to rate and share your review.

Thank you!